The Yellow Table

The Yellow Table

Alicia Stubbersfield

*For Gill
with my best wishes
for your writing.
Alicia
The Hurst, April 2015*

Pindrop Press

Published 2013 by
Pindrop Press
Mallards
Steers Place
Hadlow
Kent

www.pindroppress.com

Copyright © Alicia Stubbersfield, 2013

ISBN 978-0-9573290-1-0

Alicia Stubbersfield hereby asserts her moral right to be identified as the author of this book in accordance with the Copyright, Designs and Patents Act of 1988. All rights reserved.

A catalogue record for this book is available from the British Library.

Typeset by Pindrop Press.

Printed and bound in the UK by Lightning Source.

Cover: 'Kate's Flowers', oil on plywood, Winifred Nicholson, 1929-1936. Reproduction courtesy of The Art Gallery, New South Wales. Copyright held by The Winifred Nicholson Trust.

Acknowledgements

Acknowledgements are due to the editors of the following publications where some of these poems, or versions of them, first appeared:

Magma, The Rialto, Smith's Knoll, In the Red, blankpages, The North, Best of Manchester Poets Vol 2, Drey.

Poetry Pool 4, edited by Gladys Mary Coles & Aileen La Tourette, Headland Press, 2008.

'Lights in the Harbour' was shortlisted for The Bridport Prize 2010.

'Keeping the Creases' was shortlisted for The Bridport Prize 2011.

My heartfelt thanks to Sam Willetts and Dean Parkin for their painstaking reading of these poems and for their advice which was so astute and wise.

Gratitude is also due to Emily Wills, Jenny Newman, Aileen La Tourette, Paul Magrs, Off the Page and Cherington Poets for their perceptive support.

For Joe

Contents

More Musicians

Stone, 15
Lazarus, 16
Frozen, 17
Just Changing the Car, 18
Eaten Cake is Soon Forgotten, 19
My Ex-Mother-in-Law, 21
Hornets, 22
The Prescription, 23
November, 24
March, 25
Yorkshire, 26
Sunday Morning, 27
Valentine's Day, 28
Viper's Bugloss, 29
Out of the Blue, 30
Miles Away, 31
Over, 32
More Musicians, 33

Marking

Primary School, 37
With the Grain, 38
Marking, 39
Year 7, Period I, Wednesday, 40
Danielle and Kerry, 41
Hearing Voices, 42
Keeping it Back, 43
Shane, 44
Scream, 45
The Game, 46
Jack, 49
Relatives' Group, 50
Lights in the Harbour, 51

Influenced

Change the buttons and you get away with it…, 55
In Need of Some Updating, 56
The Yellow Table, 57
Influenced, 58
Afterlife, 59
Red Windcheater, 60
Listening to Ruby Tuesday. 61
Alice-in-Wonderland Display, Llandudno, 1960, 62
Silk Kimono, 63
Under the Skin, 64
Another Test, 65
Dimming, 66
The Space, 67
McDonald's, Darlington, 68
September, 69
Keeping the Creases, 70
Leaving for the Convent, 71
Not Letting Go, 72
Southern Belle, 74
Blood in Nashville, 75
Above the Roof Terrace, 76

More Musicians

Stone

Chosen from that beach.
Fine black lines scribbled
in a language I half-understand.

The pebble fits, weights my pocket.
I turn it like runes or dice or worry
beads, hope it has a message.

Sideways it's a face, eyes blind,
a future buffeted, waves sometimes
eighty feet high. Sucked in, shuffled out.

Stone – not shell. No faraway tide sound,
no ocean-memory or lost sea-creature.
Basalt, smooth as someone's skin.

Lazarus
after Joseph Epstein's sculpture

You look coyly over
your shoulder, standing up,
wanting admiration for this trick,
your bandages coming loose,
body not quite ready.

Last time you were hidden
in a black box, tied with red ribbon,
an artist's installation
returning you to the solitude,
relief perhaps, of being dead.

Undone again, box cracking
open like a huge, black egg,
the fragile chick of your body
staggering from death's shell
into the chapel's light and air.

An overdose resuscitated,
the boy cut down too soon,
mouth-to-mouth filling lungs
with someone else's breath,
dawn's yellow slipping through.

I know that place, waking
from anaesthetic, still in dream,
hearing a stranger's voice soothing,
bright like winter-flowering cherry.

Frozen

In this blue dress I am water
eddying round your questions like rocks.

Water freezes,
lets everything slide over its glassiness.

For years our goldfish survived icy winters
by swimming far enough below the pond's surface.

Under the ice
grief's small creature still quivers its fins.

Just Changing the Car

Too many miles, seats embossed
with dog hair, dent in the roof
where boys played a game,
walking over cars in the night.

We bought it for my fiftieth
when I'd told you I was leaving.
You haggled over the price,
gave me what I wanted.

Pale-green Micra, matching
seats and steering-wheel,
a woman's car, small enough
to clean easily, to manoeuvre.

Now I'm sitting here, doing a deal
on my own. A dark-blue Almera,
three years old, five doors, Sat Nav
so I know where I'm going.

Eaten Cake is Soon Forgotten

I could have made you cake,
the Victoria sponge I learned
in Domestic Science.
It would have taken
all afternoon, measuring, sifting,
breaking free-range eggs
into a soft puff of flour.
Then creaming using Granny's
wooden spoon – splintery
and a bit chutney-stained –
best for changing it all into
a smooth dropping consistency.

When we lived in Yorkshire
the Aga would've needed
plenty of coal and the wind
in the right direction to heat
it up for long enough to bake
a cake into a sweet, light cloud.
Not like that Christmas cake
I *did* make, burnt round the edges,
the special green glacé cherries
tasting just like red ones.

You wouldn't have been home
in time for afternoon tea
served on china from my first
marriage, the Portmeirion flowers
you didn't want when we divorced –
fair enough – you bought plain white
when you set up house alone.
There would be cake forks
like the ones our son learned to use
in cafés with his grandmother
on days out in York.

The cake is uneaten, perfect

on a white doily ready for
no-one's knife to slice it evenly.

My Ex-Mother-in-Law

They're scattering her ashes on Saturday,
probably in the Goyt Valley
where she escaped from city and family
into her own tiny caravan,
the green of trees, a cuckoo calling.

Home became the smell of old lard,
overcooked chops and mashed potato
kept hot in the hostess trolley.
It was the Ercol, the shag-pile carpet, brown
and orange 70s curtains, a bottle of Bailey's
and that photograph of her first husband,
brought out after my father-in-law died.

Upstairs, grime darkened the peach bath,
the hoist stretched like a bandage across it,
crystal animals dusty on the dressing table.

Only once she spoke to me
about her second marriage,
how she'd stopped trying
to discuss things with him.
Fifty years together: separate
bedrooms, his trips to Paris alone,
her dancing and the bridge parties.

No-one else, no lover – just the past celebrated
each February. Their daughter driving her along
the same quiet lanes a young man and his girl
cycled together, before the war.

Hornets

The sound they made was like rain,
or cellophane crackling
as the nest grew, layer on layer,
cream and brown, striated, fragile,
full of insects' agitation.

At night they'd bang against our windows,
their big yellow bodies crawling on glass.
Two or three would helicopter round
a lampshade, slower than wasps,
easier to catch in a cup, put out again.

The pest-control man came
in an unmarked van,
his white suit protecting him
as he gassed them with a long pipe.

The constant in-and-out stopped,
bodies dotted on the barn floor.
Nights quiet, just the softness of moths.
Months later I knocked the nest down,
crumbled burnt-paper artwork into dust.

The Prescription
*for Dr. Anne Griffiths, after an article in **The Guardian**,*
9th August 2005, suggesting that G.P.s should prescribe dogs

So when are you going to get a dog?
I'm in for a check-up, not many months
after finishing chemo, my hair growing,
exercises and time at the gym –
I can raise my arm above my head.

I mutter about puppies and my son
wanting a whippet. Two days later
her voice on my answer machine,
There's a whippet puppy at the Dog Rescue.

Joe and I go to see him, not quite whippet,
but lurcher-beautiful, his cartoon ears,
pointy nose, kangaroo legs as he jumps up.
He's the colour of a pale conker, just as shiny.

I walk in all weathers, mark changes
by the coming of swallows, an adder
sunning itself or the fat black of berries.
I say hello to the man in a Santa hat
walking his dog on Christmas Day.

Better than Tamoxifen to thwart cancer's return,
or Prozac to ward off the slow sadness of age,
Stanley leaps to meet me, his whole body pleased.

November

This year's first sleety snow
pinches my cheeks, leaves
tiny flakes on my eyelashes.
The hill and sky are grey,
evened out into quiet.

No other dogs, just Stanley,
stopping now and then to shake
off a cold layer or smell cowpats
like Christmas puddings
decorated with berries.

Icy air sharpens my senses,
dispels work's claustrophobia.
I walk on snow's fragile page,
write my progress across it,
not looking as it melts back to mud.

March

Rabbits on the hill have been enticed
from darkness as I am into my garden
where I dig dead leaves into sandy soil
and watch worms squirm then disappear.
A thrush waits in the plum tree until I go.

I remember our cockerels that first fine
spring day, standing up to each other:
all beak and claw and iridescent feathers
until one dragged himself away,
blood on the still-cold earth.

Gold Cup week in Cheltenham,
the buzz of it – kids I taught asking
who I was betting on, Jamie coming in
with a wad of money after bunking off.

I still think about March 1998
when I lay on the sofa, waiting,
while the final chemo raced through my veins.

Yorkshire

Curlews hurtled over the hill
the first spring we lived in Yorkshire,
their calling round our house, marking
out home, and me watching: silent, amazed.

Tornado jets re-sprayed
the colour of desert sand
cut through the same bit of sky,
practising for the Gulf.
Joe, six years old, thinking war
was here, in our field with us
in the firing line, collateral damage
like some other parent and child would be.

My mother, Madame Defarge,
knitting in the corner, watched
the television's guillotine, shocked
at what they let us know – she still
subject to the Official Secrets Act,
after her time at Bletchley Park.

Each first week of March, curlews
spun their web of sound, although
I never saw them arrive again –
just heard wild spirals of bird cry,
males showing off what they could do.

Sunday Morning

The church bells' soft clamour
rises into circles widening
like ripples from a stone.

Birdsong fills newly-hidden branches,
bands of light make geometry
on the woods' dry floor.

Rabbits scutter, a deer's spiky
silhouette stays on the ridge
a moment before bounding away.

May sun touches my skin,
polishes the dog's fine fur
as we walk the white road.

One magpie tearing at road kill
is not necessarily an omen.

Valentine's Day

This year I'm doing something
different with my heart

holding it in my own cupped hands
watching it swell again

like the Chinese paper flower
I put in water as a little girl

waiting for it to open slowly
bloom into a great peony

filling the whole glass
with layers of tissuey petals.

Viper's Bugloss

And later, the blue of viper's bugloss:
lilac-pink turning to Greek blue,
blue as the Aegean Sappho leapt into
after climbing a limestone path
like this one on Crickley Hill.

Spiked lanterns of blue, not the purple
of Lawrence's gentians lighting his way
into the dark but as good at holding it back.

Imagine their persistence, year after year,
the tenacity required to push through
hard earth, stony soil. The slow opening.

Harvest these small flowers, infuse,
for a *decoction to assist mother's lactation*
or leave them where they are:
fragments of sky, splinters of sea, far inland.

Out of the Blue
Andrew Logan's sculpture and jewellery museum in Berriew
for Danasamudra

We're driving down Welsh lanes,
I'm explaining how I've always wanted
to see a kingfisher and you're saying
there are lots on the river by your house.
We arrive at the huge Biba rose
above the museum's doors.

A Hall of Mirrors, glitter, glass
refracting, reflecting. I'm the Fat Lady,
the Thinnest Lady, Picasso portrait,
my multiple personalities rainbowed
on the walls – everything is gold, silver,
a circus, theatre, fairground, the inside
of a Pharaoh's tomb, crowns and tiaras
lit with neon – The Alternative Miss Worlds
jut their hips, Divine stares at us
and we gaze inside the floating woman
filled with the Taj Mahal, with unrequited love.
We drop five pence in the Lulu Fountain,
wish for glamour, glitz, the impossible
gorgeousness of jewels and broken mirrors.

Back outside in the quiet green
I catch a high-pitched agitation,
glimpse a flitting across water:
turquoise gleam, bright enough
to pin on a tranny's frock.

Miles Away

I'm spreading my profile onto the screen:
*I like country walks with my dog, the sea,
dry white wine, reading. I have a GSOH.*

Prospero 45 replies and I'm intrigued,
as much by his name as the information.

I remember The Library Theatre 1969,
the first Prospero I ever saw: father,
wizard, glitter falling on the stage.

I tick *Sorry I was miles away*
in the *More About You* section.

I compare what men find attractive:
always *long hair, showing affection in public,*
never *tattoos or sarcasm.*

A photo comes through,
an ordinary, balding fifty-year-old.
Then another – of his foot – he says
it *looks thirty-five.*

My friend says my attitude is wrong,
I should think of it as a project. Have fun.

Another suggests I write poems about them.
A sequence perhaps? I find *Managing
My Profile* and click *Remove*.

Over

*Remember it's been part of you
for five years – expect some blood.*
I have counted out my life
in intrauterine devices.

The first at twenty-five,
a teacher, away from my mother.
The harassed Family Planning doctor
asking if I was the last, dropping
the Copper 7, having to start again.

In Manchester they changed them
when you were bleeding – the cervix
soft and open – in Yorkshire it was different.
They wouldn't like that here.

Out for the baby, then in again,
one doctor wearing green plastic gloves
showing them to me as I lay, legs akimbo.
It was Valentine's Day 1987.

I lie here, staring at the kitten poster,
my coil is gently tugged out
by the trainee GP, *It looks fresh,*
he says and I feel obscurely pleased
as though I'd kept it nice on purpose.

More Musicians

First line of *Suzanne* and I'm there,
in that living-room and your father saying
What's this? picking up my new copy
of Leonard Cohen's poems, reading *Suzanne*
in his Polish accent, weighting word after word
until it makes no sense. *What's this?*

There's nothing to say because it's not the poem
he's asking about, it's us
and we don't know the answer.
What did I know then about love or sex?
I lost my virginity neatly enough to your friend:
I remember you outside his house, calling my name.

You email me one August after twenty years:
I email back. You have missed me. I reply you don't
know who I am any more so how can you miss me?
We walk my dog. You have no children, took early
retirement and must be home before your wife.
You buy me a torch because I light up your life again.

When you say you'd rather spend the time in bed,
I know why I went to town with him that afternoon,
left you feeling sorry for yourself. At home, I play *Suzanne*
from the new live album: more musicians, not so plaintive
and the purple Maglite shines its narrow beam on the past
where, in your mind, we've always been lovers.

Marking

Primary School

My peg marked with the strawberry
I chose on that first morning,
a green and white bag
for indoor or outdoor shoes,
always Clarks, laces impossible
to untie with my bitten nails.
A seat next to the first black boy
I'd ever seen, a G.I.'s son from the base,
the strange, scented sweets he gave us.

Dining-hall patrolled by Mrs. Bolton,
morning milk going off in chubby bottles.
My apron pocket was a mess
of mushy peas by the end of each week.
Thurstan Tyrer sick into his plate.
Wendy and I made to sit there until
we'd finished tapioca, sago, semolina.

Upstairs the nursery, classrooms,
bathroom where other people
queued for cod liver oil from a spoon.
Mrs. Whalley threw chalk,
Mrs. Rathbone rapped knuckles
if we got our sums wrong.
Mondays dancing with Miss Deacon,
Miss Maher for elocution – *Father's car
is a Jaguar,* calling me a *rude little girl.*

Friends Reunited has four names
from all those years of children.
No-one wants to be reminded
of outside toilets, gristle in the stew,
pages of copying from the board,
Elizabeth wetting her knickers,
made to sit on a newspaper
on the stairs for hours.
Small acts of humiliation every day.

With the Grain

Science was the smell of burning,
of gas leaking, high arched taps
to flick water at your friend when
the teacher's back was turned,
an ancient foetus preserved in a bottle,
my rat floating through formaldehyde,
yellowing and pinned-out, lesson
after lesson, for months.

The comforts of Domestic Science.
Miss Wright – *Pens poised girls* – teaching us
to *réchauffe,* her directoire knickers
clasping fat knees. Slow afternoons
ending in the scrubbing of pine tables –
With the grain, girls – a gondola basket filled
with that night's tea carried home on the bus.

Maths was Miss Stabler insisting on a sharp pencil,
neat lines, the beauty of geometric precision.
Four tries to get 'O' Level:
the humiliation of Mr Jones throwing
my test papers on the floor, making me
do a simultaneous equation on the board
and the whole class laughing.
Mr Harding, whose kindness saved me.

Mrs Brough for five years – *Je m'appelle Sylvie.*
Ouvrez les fenêtres. Voilà les falaises de Dieppe.
Her stacked shoe, bent back, bright green eyes,
blonde hair, telling us how to deal with men –
Make them believe they've thought of it –
passing round blue mascara in 1967:
boys silent on the other side of the classroom.

Marking

Piles of exercise books next to my chair,
the oily smell of them, the stickiness
of Year 9 pages. Red pens – standard
issue biros or uniballs bought as a treat.

Years of using pencil or green or black
because red was negative, belittling, unkind,
tempered by smiley-face stickers or gold stars.

Long explanations at the end of their work,
called feedback now and available asap,
certainly within twenty-one days though
we know all students want is the grade.

Moderation arguments over those grades
and levels, criteria and personal response.
What, exactly, is a Level 5?

Average we're told. Not Daniel, a Level 3/4,
barely able to read jolly instructions on what
he must do to climb the blue ladder at the side
of the grid and reach the thumbs-up.

He knows he's a sad-face sticker,
but he's a good footballer, a good Catholic,
is shocked at those of us who don't believe.

Year 7, Period 1, Wednesday

The girl at the front says
she wants to cut my head off.
I ask her if I would carry it
under my arm like one of Henry's wives
or stand in front of the class,
my neck spurting blood.
She turns away, bored already.

I imagine her stuffing it into her bag
like the boy's book she said
she intended to burn later,
telling the R.E teacher to fuck off
when he tried to get it back.

Her red hair glints,
she played the dragon in our story,
reading her part with feeling.
She's had years in care,
a mother who comes and goes.

I stick gold stars in her book
for pages of unintelligible writing,
for not swearing directly at me,
for staying in her seat most of the time,
for cutting off bits of herself.

Danielle and Kerrie

Danielle is pregnant for the third time in a year,
living with her boyfriend's mate
after her glamorous mother chucked her out –
said she put a hex on all her relationships.

She's next to Kerrie who has chosen to be deaf,
who me-maws, never knows what I've said.
The lads shout her name or *Fatty*,
tell me it doesn't matter as she won't hear anyway.

They think I can't see them texting under the table
or writing notes to each other, giggling at reams
of jumbled sentences about other girls doing it,
about hating their mothers and needing chocolate.

The abortion is next week – *no hurry*, the doctor said.
Twelve weeks before you have to make up your mind.
I'm not supposed to, but I tell her to get on with it.

Hearing Voices

10P5 stares at me horrified
You hear voices Miss?

I explain – not voices exactly,
not speaking outside my head
but a discussion with myself.
What might happen if I do this
                              or that,
what my mother would say:

You've made your bed, now…
just what we didn't want to happen,
don't wear white shoes in winter.
He's just a great I am.

Steve is anxious, Becky giggles.
Mostly they look blank, or bored.

I try to imagine my head empty,
how I might behave without rehearsals,
without knowing what my mother, my granny,
or even 10P5 would think.

Keeping it Back

For once the hall is quiet,
Year 11 is ready for one of its own.
The thin boy sits at the piano,
his flat mohican yellow under lights.

Long fingers coax note
after note, even Kieran farting
is lost in the swell of sound.

This is the boy teachers must not
be alone with ever. Who, after being sent
away, jokes with his mates about the psychiatric
unit, his madness, his mutable sexuality,
rubbing up against laughing boys and girls.

He's had no music lessons,
no playing of scales day after day,
no training in composition.

His music is the flame he kindled –
we don't know how – then watched
as it licked furniture, books, curtains
growing scarlet, orange, yellow until
it burned his family's house down.

Shane

Shane comes in late, nods at me,
stares out of the window.
What's that miss? The light's weird.
It's a Bible illustration or Blake showing us
God pointing out something on The Malverns.

Shane notices, in the way he noticed
the pattern and glitter of chewing-gum
on tarmac below my classroom.

He picks up the 'Of Mice and Men' worksheet,
discusses with his mate how to get tonight's weed
then gazes, again, past the school buildings,
watches the afternoon light solarise Cleeve Hill.

I tell him he has an artist's eye.
Miss, I don't get on with Mr. Perry.
I just sit at the back in art and do nothing.

Scream

Not even Halloween but Dan is wearing his Scream mask,
filing in with the rest of the class who are pointing, giggling,
Miss, Miss, look at Dan… I ignore them and him.

He sits in his place, the place I have assigned him in my plan,
where he is out of the way of anyone he might want to annoy,
quite near the back of the room but within my sight line,

I give out books, discuss marks and how to fill in some sheet
or other which requires skills of self-reflection, the desire
to improve and move from a Level 5 to Level 6 or 3 to 4.

Everyone settles down. Dan needs a pen so I lend him one,
ask him not to write anything rude on the cover of his book.
The white rubber Ghostface nods and starts on a clean page.

The Game

1.

Nothing stops me he said, and told me
how to keep a piece of razor blade
under a thumb nail, ready to slice
the house alarm wire, how to balance
on furniture round a room, avoid
heat-sensitive rays. He could spot plain-clothes
security, knew where to steal cashmere,
wore designer labels before anyone else.

The game was to break in when people slept,
to gather jewellery from a dressing-table
in silence – even a charm bracelet – so the sleepers
in the bed would not wake, see him slip out again,
cartoon-tip-toe down the stairs,
lift the door chain like the wire-loop game.
Sometimes he'd find car keys, get away
in a purring Mercedes or BMW.

He got caught, more than once.
At fourteen did time in Wetherby.
They run the lads on the racecourse
so they come out fit and strong.
He helped me move house,
carried marble-tops from washstands,
boxes of books, all on his own.

Much later it was drugs. Not petty dealing,
the big stuff – a cartel, multi-millions,
everything hidden in crates of car parts,
imported from France and Belgium.
He was regional manager.
Went down for twenty years.

I remember visiting him in Stockport Police cells.
He was about fifteen. We spoke through bars.
I had to show the sergeant the apples, Dairy Milk,

a book – *Confessions of a Window Cleaner* –
before I gave them to him. Afterwards I couldn't forget
his pale, closed face, his white shirt hanging over his jeans.

2.

I don't know how it started, he must've asked,
half-joking, if he could come round and I said yes.
Saturday mornings he'd sit at my kitchen table,
mug of tea, chocolate biscuit, not speaking for ages,
me chatting on and on, until, suddenly, all the stories.

About twelve or thirteen then. A bit older when
his probation officer rang, asked if I could help.
He wouldn't talk in their sessions, just silence
clanging its iron gate between them. I wrote letters
every time he went to court, explained his intelligence
how he needed education, exams, possibilities.

His mother had run off to Aberdeen, taking his sister,
his university lecturer father left ironic notes for his son,
stammered at Parents' Evening, played croquet for Cheshire.
He stole cars. Drove a Fiat Uno round to my house
when I'd bought a white one, abandoned it two streets away.

We lost touch, though I went to his wedding,
met his son only two months younger than mine.
Lorry-driving was never going to be enough.
Nearly twenty years later, BBC news described
the *sophisticated and professional* business
he helped to run, £58,000 cash in his *luxury* flat,
crack cocaine, cannabis. He dealt on a *truly massive scale*.

What stories will he tell now? If he speaks at all,
if he writes the kind of letters he wrote as a boy
from one Young Offenders' Institution after another.
Pages and pages of clear writing describing his life:
the mates he made, how to get the newest shirts,
how things would be different when he came out.

Jack

A gambler, winning the house and land at poker,
coming home in someone else's Mercedes
after a night playing cards, doing a deal.
At shows your daughters hid their horses
so you couldn't be reminded, use them as collateral.

You were calm enough to make men parachute out
of planes, to clear Auschwitz after the war. I dived
under water, picked up a brick when you trained
the pentathlon team. *It's only money* you said,
now you had plenty after years working in St Helens'
chip shops and the welding factory, still washed
and shaved in the kitchen, embarrassing your wife
who tolerated unmarked saddles in the hall,
boxed crystal cigarette lighters piled up, strange visitors.

The cortege mapped St Helens' narrow streets.
We drank your favourite *La Flora Blanche,*
told stories about you and laughed.
You'd said life wouldn't be worth living without a deal:
the wad in your back pocket just ready to peel,
notes pressed into a hand before you shook on it.

Relatives' Group

Straight-backed National Health chairs in a circle upstairs,
downstairs, the A.A. meeting we don't see or hear about.
Relatives take their places again, ready to exchange
another week's anger, fear and tales of mad deceit.

The young woman hesitates at the door but comes in,
begins to explain how her fiancé promised never to drink
again, how the odd sherry couldn't do any harm, could it,
and how she'd change him when they married.

We lean forward, Mary whose husband was morbidly
jealous, who had four children under five and was pregnant,
Sandy, whose husband was a binge-drinker going away
for days at a time, coming home with roses, promises.

The same promises Ian's wife made each time
she stopped the whisky, before she began again. We
lean forward and say *No. No. Don't even think about it.*
Mary strokes her belly's curve. *Get out while you can.*

The girl looks at her tiny solitaire, twiddles it on her finger.
I love him, she says and spikes our tongues.

Lights in the Harbour

After the Alcohol Treatment Unit Relatives' Meetings
we'd dash to The Albert, order a pint and a gin & tonic
to prove to ourselves we were ok, we could have just
the one and walk away relaxed, made more sociable.
We didn't have to pretend that morning gin was water,
or hide bottles in cisterns, fill hoses in the garage with
cheap whisky, throw empties into neighbours' gardens,
unlike our relatives who'd been downstairs at A.A.
who were binge drinkers, drip-drinkers topped-up
all day and most of the night.

Another? No thanks, I say, watching the man
at last orders carry two pints back to his table
and fumble out a coin to put *Sea of Heartbreak*
on the juke box.

Influenced

Change the buttons and you'll get away with it...

Buttons run through your fingers,
not-quite-sand on the West Shore,
small, cool pebbles ground by sea.

Imagine the garments, long gone
to dusters or given to the rag-and-bone
man calling down our street.

Pick some out – one a fifties beaded hat
my aunt wore going back to Nashville,
her baby son in her arms.

This the perfect bow my mother tied
into my pin-curled hair, arranging me
for the photograph.

Here is the Art Deco bathroom at our hotel,
black tiles and green bath, basin:
I can be Esther Williams.

Now the ocean beyond our window,
storm-churned, cloud-edged by lightning,
mother-of-pearl moon hidden.

This one is the story's pink gleam,
an ammonite uncurling dreams.

In Need of Some Updating

This was my house with the red-tiled porch
my mother polished with Cardinal not very often,
where swallows returned year after year,
fledglings bulging over the nest edge
inches from our back door. The water-tower
like a fairy castle beyond the garden,
next to the railtrack where Huskisson was killed
by Stephenson's *Rocket* on its first trip.

The house where I didn't contradict
and learned spellings for a test on Friday,
read pony books and kept myself to myself.
My bedroom at the front with the window
covered by a Venetian blind after I climbed out
to talk to the milkman's horse.

In the kitchen chutney bubbled,
Granny spoke Spanish or Scottish
and all the sadness was held at bay.
Here my mother made my mini dresses,
one a week for 60s discos and copping off
by ten o'clock, Cherry B or Babycham,
and knowing what nice girls didn't do.

I find it for sale on Right Move,
take the 360 degree virtual tour.
I'm not there in the dining-room
watching telly, my mother isn't sewing
at the kitchen table, my father is not telling
my mother to leave him alone
as he crumples on the hall floor
where I am no longer crying inconsolably
when the cat is lost, a year after he died.

The Yellow Table

My mother's defiance of post-war monochrome,
splayed legs sturdy on the lino's primary colours,
four matching chairs made of squashy plastic.
All wipe-clean, mid-century-modern surfaces.

My cousin from America swung back on his chair
until he fell, biting through his lip against the table edge.
My mother and her new friend drank wine and laughed
in the kitchen, making clothes for Audrey's dances at the Ritz.

The table came with my mother when she moved in with us,
we took it to Cheshire, Yorkshire and, after she died, to Wales.
When we divorced I kept it in my garage, the yellow smudged
from all the kitchens I'd painted, fifty years' wear and tear.

Now I'm throwing it away. No point imagining eBay auctions
or doing it up. I unscrew four pale-oak legs, the extending flaps
from each end and place the top along the skip side,
yellow Formica facing outwards, still gaudy, still doing its best.

Influenced

This book spills open, slipping like milk
down steps to the garden path,
scattering crumbs through the forest
taking me somewhere I don't know
with people I will come to know or become.
Who am I today, tomorrow?

Read 'The Rainbow' twenty years later
and it's not the same novel.
My father's books have his name handwritten
on the flyleafs or gold-embossed,
St Francis Xavier's school prizes,
then the Clement's Inn Prize.

All his family were readers and I belong
to the Saki story he read me
about the girl who won medals for goodness,
was eaten by wolves. Better not strive too hard
to be the nice girl my mother wanted.

This book by the side of my bed
or that one in the pile for the charity shop:
each deceives with its quiet, solid weight.
Each one tumults, is a packet of seeds,
a wound you can never dress.

Hold the torch under the bedclothes.
Ruin your eyes.
Join the spectacle-wearing dreamers
away with the fairies.

Afterlife

God will have found a way
said my great-aunt, a nun
for fifty years and sure
my father's immortal soul
would be saved.

In our bathroom,
bottles of holy water
sent from relatives on trips
to Lourdes were left
to turn green, untouched.

No miracles for us,
not in that winter of '63
when my father fell,
broke his leg, bled internally,
secretly, for hours.

No last rites performed
in his hospital room,
though his family prayed outside,
my mother's Presbyterian anger
razor wire round his bed.

He did not suddenly turn back,
on that Easter Sunday,
to the God he thought
had abandoned him.
What a wonderful day to die.

Red Windcheater

I suppose my mother threw out his suits –
no charity shops in 1963 –
kept only his Sam Browne belt,
the scarlet, navy and gold Royal Artillery cap.

He said he bought nothing – *The Liverpool Echo*
and his suits. Two a year, tailored
by Werners of Bold Street. One tweed
for weekends, one weekday dark.

He wore gleaming shoes,
always the same style, one pair black,
the other ox-blood, polished with Kiwi,
(not Cherry Blossom) and spit.
He taught me how.

When I saw him in hospital that last time,
zipped into a red windcheater,
I stood in the doorway, smelt disinfectant,
stared at my lace-ups' shine.

Listening to *Ruby Tuesday*

There's something about that gay light that draws you.
you say, and I wonder what that *gay light* is
in your eyes as you look at me and we begin to laugh.

It began at eighteen, my first lover took my virginity
with the lightest touch, drew me in a 1930s gown,
bought me anemones and left me for a window-dresser.

We were all in love with Bowie then, weren't we?
Swapping our velvet trousers, eyes made-up sultry,
everyone knew pretty boys had the most luck.

I've slept with one or two more who wondered what
they really fancied – I was *gamine, androgynous*
wanted to be Julie Driscoll or *Ruby Tuesday*.

Life *was* unkind and I'd always known it. My father knew it.
Back from Dunkirk and everything else he didn't talk about,
glad I was a girl so I'd never have to go to war.

I was drawn to his light too. Everything he told me:
The Magic Flying Carpet, Kemal Attaturk, the laws
of trespass to explain the sign outside Piglet's house.

With you now, I feel as light as I did when I was a girl,
laughing at something no-one else will think is funny,
on the edge of everything possible and dangerous.

Alice-in-Wonderland Display, Llandudno 1960

Hidden in Happy Valley, Alice is Bakelite,
taking tea with The Mad Hatter, machinery
jerks her round to The White Rabbit's seat.

I'm allowed to stay up, to see the figures
illuminated in soft, sea-side dark.
I'm walking through a book at last.

Caterpillar glows on his red and white toadstool,
gazes at me, smokes hookah dreams
while cat eyes loom from the chestnut tree.

Darkness settles into corners, purring quietly,
the characters are brighter now. I'm squashed
with Alice, our feet sticking out of a chimney.

My mother and I walk back along the promenade,
the pier is alive with strolling couples, groups
of boys and girls, a neon sign: *The Beverley Sisters*.

A walrus and a carpenter cavort on the beach,
I swing my croquet stick, watch a hedgehog scuttle,
hear my mother shout *Off with his head.*

Silk Kimono

Draped over my dressing-table,
a spill of fuchsia, green and white
reflected in the mirror
while Teddy and Carol Bear sit and wait.

Granny stands behind me, half-afraid,
still hearing me scream, still running
down the hall to find me,
her helpless vomiting as Mum drove
to the surgery, my hand wrapped in a towel.

I know what to say. Thank her
as she slips it over the bandage,
wraps the wide sash round my waist.
My face pale above bright flowers.

I still take the kimono away with me
in case the bathroom's down the hall.
Just a sliver of silk from Warrington market,
the pattern Granny drew in chalk,
cut out, sewed with all those tiny stitches:
just a jacket now, folding into nothing.

Under the Skin

Feel this she says, rolling up her jumper.
I recoil and try not to show it, touch soft,
saggy skin and a ball-bearing under it.

It's only a small one I say, helping to pull
down the blue jumper. My mother restored
before her next round of hospital trips.

Years later, my lump was much bigger, flatter.
Mobile, the locum said, *a good sign.* Deceptive
as it turned out, wrapped in benign tissue

like pass-the-parcel with no treat at the centre
only my own bead, pea, marble, tumour
surprise, the one out of ten not *all right*.

My mother and I didn't touch much,
she reckoned I rejected her from the first,
her milk too rich then too thin.

A baby photo shows her holding me away
from her body as I smile into the camera
at my father who hugged easily and often.

Eventually we were paired up. Mastectomies:
hers right, mine left. Not that we would have
compared even if we'd been able to.

Another Test

I read the result of my mammogram,
dictated, not signed to speed delivery.
My Amazon breast *shows satisfactory*
appearances with no cause for concern.

The registrar writes he *is happy to tell me,*
I am happy to take the news
into spring sun on Leckhampton Hill.

My dog and I scramble up
a disappearing path, he spots rabbits
while I clutch at stones, clumps of grass.
Violets spread themselves, unexpectedly bright.

I have no cause for concern,
like the Tarot Fool on the brink of something,
stepping out in yellow with his dog and a flower.

I watch light soften the motorway
as it cuts through fields, right across
to the Malverns' dark spine,
below us, Cheltenham glinting like bone.

Dimming
for Linda Chase

When you died, trees were newly rich
and late daffodils blew their own trumpets.
My dead jostled for position, trying to line up
in order of importance: father, mother, granny,
best friend and my pony, Sam, whinnying
down the years. They elbowed each other
trying to remind me. I do remember them
like I remember you telling me of old lovers,
new poems and on that Wednesday,
when you knew you were going to die,
saying *I've had an idea.*

Soon enough they faded:
let go my imagination, moved back
into those slanted places, memory's
dimmer switch turned down again.

The Space

Empty bed, duvet pushed to the side.
How you left it. Sheet wrinkled, pillow
still dented by your sleepless head.

Your mother cannot strip it, cannot
gather up stale laundry, shove it into
the washer. She kneels, smells you.

A week since you planned everything,
carried all you needed in a rucksack
to the spot you'd chosen near school.

Carefully planned like essays you wrote,
graffiti, all your art. But, until this one final
act, never quite perfected enough for you.

Inside the wicker coffin now; a too-big
Moses basket to take you back. A space
in Film Studies, the art room; your guitar silent.

That veil of drizzle as we leave church,
a rainbow like Christmas paper chains
over the five hundred mourners filing out.

The church gate is suddenly smokers' corner
as kids huddle, desperate, heads down, hiding.
Your friend with his angel ringlets, his aged eyes,

trying to make sense of it, dressed in black
and maroon like everyone, made helpless
by your mother's blame, his own imagination.

You smile from the Order of Service. We fold
it into pockets and bags, take it home. Keep safe.
One day we'll open it out, see you unchanged.

MacDonald's, Darlington

His paper bag turns him into The Elephant Man,
I am not a monster. I am a human being.
Mates around the table splutter and laugh.

The Darlington Echo said addicts shoot up
in the toilets here. Probably not at twelve noon,
the room full of children, Happy Meals, mothers.

My son eats chicken nuggets with his fingers,
I drink the too-sweet Coke he hates but came free.
He sips fresh orange, no bits, from the waxed cup.

A mother drags her screaming daughter into the ladies,
another carts a baby, its reeking nappy leaves a vapour trail.
Crack cocaine wouldn't stand a chance against this lot.

Joe plays with Donatello, Raphael: Ninja turtles
defending their box on the table. My burger is damp,
slippery with gherkin, washed down with flat Coke.

The Elephant Man is restored, thin-faced, acned,
saying *fucking right*. The baby squishes chips.
You hate it here. Don't you, Mum? says Joe.

September

Fields and woods already tarnished,
blackberries and sloes remind us
of winter evenings, curtains drawn,
the lamps lit and the closing in.

Back to School in the shops, offers
on pencil cases, Teflon-coated trousers,
3-for-2 polo-shirts and grey socks.

We took photographs: the uncomfortable shorts,
acrylic jumper, his awkward smile. I left him
in the classroom easily, not like all those guilty
nursery years. Other mothers crying; stay-at-home
mums with stay-at-home children wailing.

When I collected him at the end of the day,
he said *They don't know how to share.*
Some kind of vindication for years of driving away,
the small face watching me before he turned to play.

Keeping the Creases

I'm soothing creases from black T-shirts,
obscure band names in plastic shrivelling
if I'm not careful. You tell me not to bother.
I fold them, pile up soft cotton, notice
a row of tiny holes, dark stains, a tear.

In a week's time at your father's wedding
you'll be wearing the Dolce & Gabbana suit
I haven't seen, Italian shoes, cream shirt,
red tie, all appropriate for the best man.

The first time you were away from home,
ten years old on a primary school trip,
I spent a day mending Bip, your toy clown,
darning gaps with red and blue wool,
covering his white stuffing.

He's kept in my scarf drawer. I catch a glimpse
sometimes. His arms flung out, yellow hair,
body elongated by too much loving. Even now
you ask where he is, just needing the idea of him.

Leaving for the Convent

Feel the weight of your hair,
fine Irish hair, glinting red.
Brush slowly, notice the slither
of it as you plait, twist the bun
neat at the nape of your neck.

Eat bacon and eggs with your sister,
her husband will take you to the station.
The Sacred Heart looks down.
A candle flickers on the mantlepiece,
illuminating his open wound.

Stand outside their house,
list things you want to remember:
diamond-leaded lights, dark bricks,
the willow trailing leaves, next door's
cat weaving in and out of your legs.

Walk to the station. Look back.
May is waving you off. Imagine
the tears she is wiping away.
Miners clatter past, still black
from coal dust, anxious to be home.

Jim helps you on to the train.
Katy O'Connor you look beautiful.
There is a pain in your throat.
Leave Katy O'Connor on that platform.
Sit Sister Mary Aquinas in the dingy carriage.

Not Letting Go

i.

They'd smoked a joint, drunk cider.
Were they racing? Lit by the moon
strung up above your house,
the road dry and white, the tree
solarised before he swerved, hit it,
the second car cannoned into his.

You didn't see the body, didn't
touch your son one more time.
You said you were *a basket case*,
sedated, even now taking Valium,
going over that last day, again
and again, finding no comfort.

You keep his photo out. Silver-framed,
his hippy hair blond in sunlight,
ancient pine trees frozen behind him.
In the drawer are baby clothes, a teddy,
two teenage love poems and a sympathy
letter from the girl-friend you never met.

ii.

Thirty years on and your son's friend
came to see you: *He'd found Jesus*
you said, as if reason enough
to look you up, show you photos
of his children, talk about being born again.

Yet he still needed
some kind of absolution,
some kind of grace from you.

Our family story was only about your son.
His death, the three wrecks before
the final one. The way his father – guilty
after the divorce, new wife, new baby girl –
bought car after car, each one faster.

You made your son's friend a cup of tea,
listened. Glad, I think, he had found
a way of coming to terms with that night
in 1974 when he walked away, forgotten.

Southern Belle

My aunt sits at the kitchen table,
a tray full of make-up
in front of her, the magnifying
mirror reveals each pore.

First, concealer to cover sixty
years of sun damage's spots,
then a triangular sponge dabs
foundation, smooths it over
deep wrinkles by her mouth.

The metal curler squeezes,
flicks up her eyelashes
*Most old ladies lose their lashes
as well as their hair* she says,
cleans the mascara wand,
applies layer after layer of black.

*Mary's had her eyes done twice.
My surgeon said the fat is yellow.
Bags are hereditary, you know.*
She stares at the circles under mine.

Pink outlines her still cupid's-bow lips,
she fills them in with darker pink,
puffs on blusher from a big brush.
My face is on she says, sits back,
views herself from every angle,
eighty-six years old, keeping up.

Blood in Nashville

*Bed-bugs, it'll be bed-bugs
brought by the Mexicans.*
says Hez who catches
a glimpse of my bitten legs,
the Braille of red, brilliant
against my pale Celtic skin.
I say I don't think so.

He'll hear none of it, launches
a rehearsed tirade against
immigrants who are nothing
like his immigrant ancestors:
*Not a drop of anything other
than Scottish or English blood.*

No use explaining discoveries
of African DNA in Scots.
He and my aunt would think
it a conspiracy cooked up
by Marxists like Obama.
These immigrants are *illegals,*
and shouldn't be allowed.

Soon we're on to brown recluse
spiders and how your skin
begins to necrotise, leaving
huge lesions – these can't be
blamed on Mexicans,
just evidence of the threats
around us, the need for vigilance.

In the pharmacy I ask for George
and he looks at the bites, gives me
what they had in Vietnam where
the bugs would carry you away.
I thank him, say I always get bitten
and he says, *Like my wife.
Sugar and spice, that's women.*

Above the Roof Terrace

The sky full of storks back from Mecca.
Some here already, clattering long beaks,
flinging heads back in a long S of neck.

One mounts another, her legs steady,
then they stand side-by-side, fluffing up
feathers before she pecks at him.

Soon it will be dark, too cold to stay out
here on the roof terrace with a book, oranges
like Christmas baubles on the tree in its clay pot.

For the moment, I watch these hieroglyphs-
for-the-soul doing what storks do every spring,
none ready yet to transform into their human selves

anymore than I'm ready to prepare myself
for the change into whatever it will be for me.
Just darkness probably, though some kind of bird

would be good – inhabiting the emptiness of air,
a clamour of feathers, beaks, soaring and landing
high on this wall, sun warming my stretched-out wings.